proudly presents...

PENNY PICKLES' PET POTATO

a peculiar poetry picture book

written & illustrated by
CHRIS WHITE

visit veggievampire.com

This is Penny Pickles.
Now that you have
met,
I'll tell you the reason
she looks so sad.
It's because she has
no pet.

All Penny's friends have animals
To play with, love and clean,
But Penny's parents say "NO WAY!"
Which Penny thinks is mean.

"Some bite! Some are messy!
Some are noisy!
Some smell a little bit funny!
Some leave fur all over the place!
They all cost a lot of money!"

So Penny lives her life alone
Hoping with all her might,
For a furry friend to look after
And cuddle up with at night.

Tomorrow is her birthday!
So, as she went to sleep,
Penny wished upon a star
For a pet that she could keep...

Next morning, Penny had presents!
Through the wrapping paper she tore!
A doll, a book, a plastic duck
But nothing that she had wished for...

She didn't want to seem ungrateful,
Penny sighed, "Thanks Mum and Dad."
But deep inside, she could have cried,
She was really, really sad...

Trudging across the kitchen
She headed for the door,
But Penny slipped and Penny tripped
Over something on the floor...

A smile crept across her face,
As Penny's idea came to be.
"I'll have the best pet EVER!
Just you wait and see!"

Look! Here's Danny Dinkle,
Walking down the street.
There's his cute dog, Dimples,
Trotting round his feet.

"Hi Penny! Good to see you!
What's that you've got there?
I didn't know you had a dog!"
Danny stopped...and could only
stare...

Penny skipped towards him
A very strange sight indeed.
She had a small lumpy brown thing,
Dragging behind on a lead.

"It's my brand new pet potato!" Penny yelled out loud. She picked it up to show Danny, Looking very proud.

Danny looked at the vegetable
He didn't know what to say!
As they headed to the field
Where the dogs all love to play.

Danny threw a stick for Dimples,
Dimples picked it up
Then scampered back to Danny,
"What a clever pup!"

"Go on potato! FETCH!"
Penny threw a ball through the
air
But the ball bounced into the
bushes
The potato just sat there...

Penny looked at her new pet
And sighed the deepest sigh
The potato lay there in the grass
Just staring at the sky.

Later on that very day
Penny thought she'd take,
Her potato to visit Cathy
And her pet cat, Cupcake.

Cathy had Cupcake on her knee
Softly stroking her ginger fur
Cupcake cuddled contentedly
Whilst making a happy purr.

Penny thought, "We can do that!
I can pet my pet, for sure!"
But after one stroke, he fell off
her lap
And went 'THONK!' on the floor.

"I guess my potato's the kind of pet
You can't cuddle or embrace."
Penny left Cathy and Cupcake,
A frown upon her face.

Next stop was Billy Button's house
It was Penny's wish
To show off her potato
To Billy, and Bubbles, his fish.

Billy presented Bubbles in the tank
That he had recently bought her
Whooooshing through plants and a
plastic ship,
Splashing about in the water.

Penny popped her potato in too
"Come on! Swim round the tank!"
But Penny did frown, when he
plummeted down
Her heart, like her pet...just sank.

"So you can't chase balls or be
cuddled?"
Penny said through a forced grin
"And now I've learnt something
else today,
Potatoes can't really swim."

Next it was round to
Harriet's house,
To see her hamster,
Huffy.
He scampered round
in his sawdust and
wheel
Looking all cute, small
and fluffy.

Penny put her pet on the wheel
He wobbled, then started to roll
Straight off the front and fell
with a 'FLUMP!'
Right into Huffy's food bowl.

Penny gasped, "OH NOT AGAIN!
Frustrated's how I feel!
I guess potatoes aren't cut out
To scamper on a wheel!"

"I'll take him round to Pedro's.
I hope that he might be,
Astounded and amazed,
By my little veg buddy!"

Pedro had Poppy the Parrot.
So clever, she could talk!
"Who's a pretty potato?!"
She said with a flap and a
squawk.

Polly Parrot peered at the potato.
The potato looked at the bird.
Would Penny's potato say something back?!?!?
Nope. I'm afraid, not one word.

Penny crashed down on her bed,
After sadly strolling home.
The potato lay there next to her,
Yet she still felt all alone...

"I'll always love my potato
And look after him too.
I just wish he could do the things
That other pets can do..."

As she drifted off to sleep that
night,
She had one last birthday wish.
Not for a dog or parrot or cat
Or even a hamster or fish.

She took all the love that she had
Inside her heart and head,
And wished it inside her potato,
So it could be alive instead.

In the night, strange things
happened,
As things at night often do.
Penny Pickles' pet potato
Grew and grew and grew...

He grew potaears!
He grew a potanose!
He grew a potatail!
He grew potatoes!

Did it all begin as a dream?
Where did real life start?
Or was it that good things happen
If you have good things in your
heart?

Next morning, Penny had
breakfast,
Completely unawares,
Of what was coming towards her,
Bounding down the stairs...

IT WAS HER PET POTATO!
She couldn't believe it, yet,
He jumped right up and licked her
face!
He was a proper pet!

Penny skipped along her street
And everyone ran outside,
To see her amazing petato!
Penny beamed with pride!

"IS THAT A POTATO?" someone
yelled.
"I think so. I'm not sure!
But I do know that I've never seen,
in my life,
A girl so happy before!"

So it goes to show, with a lot of love,
Plus a little wish or two,
And a splash of imagination,
You can make your dreams come true...

THE END.

Also by Chris White...

Printed in Great Britain
by Amazon